Street Images

Michael A. Susko

Published by AllrOneof Us Publishing, 2020.

STREET IMAGES

First edition. May 8, 2020.

ISBN: 979-8201797751

Written by Michael A. Susko.

Table of Contents

I dedicate this work to all those "on the street" who, through their writing, share their life and heart.

NEW INTRODUCTION TO STREET IMAGES I

As I re-read these poems, prose-poems and brief biographies, from persons I had met in my wanderings, I find I am again amazed by the poetic fire from "persons on the streets," poets and writers whose work will not grace anthologies of the future. These are persons close to the pulse of life who lived on the street, or near the street—having been placed in psychiatric in hospitals—one step removed from the streets. They are prophets in their own way, unheralded, un-noticed, but yet if we but look, we can sense their fire, hear their message. I marvel too, how in these COVID-19 times, a poet could foresee and write many years the words in a poem titled "Apocalypse."

> *While the sun goddess weeps her last song*
> *The plague has begun*
> *People in plastic bags heading toward the city dump.*
> *I lock myself in my room*

There's something evergreen about poets. Their message does not die with a given time. We need only to listen to such messages, from persons who have nothing to profit or gain from our listening. Only we stand to benefit, when we hear the resonance in our souls.

So I invite you to enter a time capsule, an eternity—where voices otherwise lost can now be heard.

Michael A. Susko, editor 5/10/2020

INTRODUCTION
TO THE ORIGINAL EDITION

The poor and those on the periphery of society are not necessarily culturally poor. "Street Persons" can harbor a rich life-story and genuine philosophic concerns. This Journal seeks to make public this hidden cultural wealth. We invited persons with hardship to create fiction or, in recounting an experience, to offer an image of hope.

The first section is written by those who are living on the streets or who once did.* The line between the streets and institutional settings becomes blurred, and thus the second section includes those who have lived in halfway houses. Last, the section entitled "End of the City" admits that nuclear weapons target the city for mass destruction. In another sense, "End of the City" hopes that the present injustice and plight will end, and a new city be born. Images of the country remind us too, that the city's boundaries end at a point, and give us relief from the streets.

Michael A. Susko, Winter, 1983

Original copyright, 1983

*Brief biographic sketches of most street authors are included in the back of the Journal.

ACKNOWLEDGEMENTS

A project such as this needs the work of many hands to complete. An early editorial staff did meet but the uncertainties that face many street persons and people in halfway houses came upon some of our members – evictions, hospitalizations, and other setbacks drew the staff apart. However, many people helped, some more at the beginning and some at the end. Thanks to Ken Rowell and Paula Romona for their participation in those early planning stages; to Harry Livingstone for his needful instigation and to Marc Grabowski who gave his time and financial support and who also proof-read the Journal. A special thanks to Blanche Van de Castle who did the bulk of the printing and having a hand in everything else, deserves an assistant editorship at least.

Institutional support was present from those who especially serve the needy. St. Ignatius Church and Bill Perkins offered hospitality to our staff at the early coffee hour and gave a donation. The Franciscan Center allowed visits to their Center and moral support, and finally Corpus Christi offered the "means of production."

Without deadlines or a boss, moral support is the sustainer and completer in such a project. Thanks to all who gave such encouragement in the slightest way.

It goes without saying that we thank the authors of this Journal who gave us more than their writings – their trust.

Finally, we acknowledge those who helped in the last hour: Larry Williams, Bob Fish, Theodore Snyder, Sally Whitener, Barbara Larcum, Cynthia Polcak, and members of the Saint Paul Half-Way House.

ON THE STREET

MEGALOPOLIS

It is hard sometimes to state precisely how one comes to understand Megalopolis: there is a Universe over our heads, but we wake up each morning and apply our finite knowledge to our life cycles. By such repetitive cycles we acquire Experience.

In terms of weakness and Susceptibility, we are tempted to believe along with Christianity in the importance of Faith as an alleviating factor. By our very nature we live by shaky, dangling threads.

And yet one questions how despite this we have been able to establish a firmament, our Civilization, with the success it has had. In the course of time, cities and countries have been destroyed for the cause of social progress. We rose above the earth.

Consider for example the Death concept. Of old things centered around the questions of War, Marriage, Justice, Men's attitudes and Death. With the emphasis on death-related issues such as these it is not surprising that Death became Symbolic.

Today we take most everything for granted. The sense of time value of our ancestors is dwindling. It's suddenly harder to bring our attention to appropriate issues. What has resulted is easily seen: the morbid attitude—life simply exists to delay Death.

It's hard to believe we allow this. How do men summon up courage, dedication, to face futurism? A question of relativity comes into play. Not surprising, therefore, is that fact that men search for other worlds, while in this one many are reduced to life in the streets.

by Bruce Whitcomb

LIFE IN THE STREETS

Every day is the same for us poor people. We have to struggle to make from day to day. We have to bum some money to eat and get everything we need.

From the time we get up in the morning, it is a struggle to live. My day is the same every day. Nothing changes at all.

The only day that changes is when I get my check. Then I have the money to get what I want.

by Red Top

MEMORY

It was a sunny day, very bright, about 90 degrees. In the sunlight by the shore, I was just getting tired of fishing. I was going to stop fishing and about one minute later, the fish got caught. It was fighting very hard, and I could hardly take him. On shore, he moved around and then got tired. I tied fishing string to his mouth and took him home.

My mother had bought fish that same day, and it was the same type I had just caught. It was a funny coincidence that happened 20 years ago.

Joe

Learn from.

the little children

the way they act

The Ball
    rolled down
    the steps
    of its
    free will
    how did it
    do it? There
    was no wind.

Lois Tragesser

MY LITTLE SPOT

My little spot weaves and bobs, walks and runs and changes in colors, hues and dimensions. For example, it can become San Francisco, Philadelphia, Milwaukee, or Chicago; it may be either autumn in Denver, with all its varying shades, or Valle after a heavy snowfall; a child walking or running across a playground; or a cork weaving and bobbing above the water as some trout swims beneath the surface.

As I awake in the morning, my little spot appears as a small speck on the wall. While I attempt to tune-in the world, it becomes clear one minute and blurry the next, until all sleep has gone from my eyes. Later it becomes a television screen, showing me the faces I must meet during the day and the places where we must meet.

During breakfast, lunch and dinner, my little spot goes over each and every item, asking that this be added and that be deleted. It demands hot food in comparison to cold and must have coffee and milk with each meal. It even blurs my vision when it thinks I have had enough or when it thinks I am eating the wrong foods.

As I leave home for work, it seems to sit next to me as I turn on the ignition, telling me when to start my automobile, when to back out of the driveway, and which route to take to work. It even, tells me where to part in the company's parking lot.

As I walk from the parking lot, my little spot seems to meet and greet all the people I pass. When I get into the office, it seems to meet and greet every employee. It generates a warm feeling even on mornings when my moods are rapidly changing.

When I answer the phone, my spot seems to go out in an attempt to view the caller and his surroundings. It usually returns with a face and the entire environment from which it comes.

As I write letters and memos during the day, it changes to varying shades. When it thinks I have chosen the wrong word, it colors the entire word lightly. When it wants a word or passage deleted, it places a dark spot above that portion.

As I leave work, my little spot leaves with me, telling me which route to take, what speed to drive at, and which lane to drive in. In this Los Angeles traffic, it takes some people an hour and a half to get home; it only takes me forty-five minutes.

Clem

ELEGY FOR A DEPARTED STREET PERSON

Lonely crumpled brown bag, and tattered trousers,
Crumpled rags, and frozen owner;
Poor soul was on the ground lying dead
Unknown to the morning traffic on the Howard Street bridge overhead.
Sun rising now to warm the chilly day,
Of no use to this man's cold, impoverished clay;
It's warmth a few hours sooner, perhaps he'd be living still.
But now the toll of cold and time had spoke its final will.
He was found by a policeman on his beat,
A priest was quickly called for last rites, given on the street
A passer-by or two stopped and stood to complete the ceremony,
His brown bag was retired now, he had completed his earthly journey.
He had lived month to month on welfare checks and soup kitchens,
He saw life in a haze, (which he denied and it him.)
His livelihood was to pound the streets; of ties completely free.
His hobbies were to find spare change, and avoid being locked up for vagrancy.
His brown bag is retired now, his faded rags are thrown away,
His memories are taken with him of street noise and balmy spring days.
His job a carefree free life with only simple comfort cares;
He traded job, house and money, for a life in the warm/cold, blow/still air.
He was classified death by freezing, job-nil, residence-none
A statistic to be added for street person's death, our hearts left cold and numb.

He was a poor beggar like St. Francis of Assisi, known as the minstrel of God. One man worshipped in a museum, the other forgotten six feet under sod.

His job was to make sense of a world gone mad.

His life was to speak of streets lovable and happy – it's a growing fad;

His heart beating self, simplicity, not rush; in one place stay.

Like him! He's a friend; winning cities his way, in our day.

Bob Fish

IS THERE ANY HOPE?

A man's toes are amputated from frostbite this winter in Baltimore. He didn't have a place to sleep in the cold, in the snow. He went to the hospital twice about it, but they didn't even take his shoes off, afraid of the stink of poverty. He needed his feet because he didn't have a car or a bus fare to get anywhere. Now he can barely walk.

The soup kitchens are busy feeding those without any food at all, something hot each day. And hot tea or coffee. Thank God for small pleasures. A cigarette, a cup of cocoa. But the necessary protein, vitamins, nutrients aren't there.

I sit up all night behind the wheel of my car, wrapped in blankets, afraid I might freeze to death. The VW is too small to lie down in. Besides, I have a large dog, and she gets to stretch out in the back seat. I want to keep her alive too. She keeps me alive in her way, for she has more love, more forgiveness, more loyalty and mere intelligence than any human. She requires so little and gives so much—my dog, one of the people.

Why go on when all hope is removed? What is there beyond bare survival and grinding poverty and fear, of terror, horror beyond words?

They want me to negate my identity, to write under a false name again, to lie, to deceive, to throw away what I have achieved. Never.

We are all born with a mission to perform. It is in our hearts. Young people who don't know why they are here haven't looked into their hearts to see what it is they must do on this earth, what their heart tells them to do, not what is expected of them. They haven't done so because the schools and their families have taken them far away from their hearts, trying to pour them into someone else's mold.

We are also born with a handicap, which is our cross to bear. Our handicap—whether sickness, poverty or even too much money—works against us when we strive to perform our mission. We must struggle to overcome our handicap as well.

Ignorance and stupidity are a great handicap and are among the most destructive forces in life, in society. All people are victims of it, or unwitting perpetrators.

There are certain forces over which we have no control. We are often in God's hands alone and we cannot help what happens to us, free will or no.

When an earthquake hits, or the sky falls in, we are not responsible. This goes for business recessions too.

I didn't choose to be a writer. I was <u>compelled</u> to write. I was born that way, telling stories. I also <u>wanted</u> to be a writer at puberty, but I <u>was</u> writing, <u>was</u> a writer. So too an artist, a sculptor. Some genius's begin fixing cars at an early age. It is in their gut. And all great minds are subject to violent opposition; Einstein said it.

"I would rather die on my feet than live on my knees," General Pancho Villa said. What do we do when we are oppressed? Some knuckle under, some fight, some are broken, some run away. Your reactions come from the gut. It's what you are. And we are all different. The Americans fought their own bloody revolution.

Now I must face death. It's closing in on me, from sickness, from age, from exhaustion. I always ran scared in this life, terrified. They did that to me as a child, along with asthma, so severe I never breathed normally a day in my life. I was so often pained for air, suffocating, that fear was built into me. I was given double and triple helpings of fear. It wasn't just sickness that made me afraid, but all of those grown-ups that tried to force a child to be something he or she is not. They try to rob you even of your soul...

Somehow we find within us that kernel, that core of what we are: our self. To let go of it, to compromise, is living death. To hold on to it, for instance to insist on being an artist when everyone does all they can to discourage you, stop you, or suppress your work, as in my case, is to take double punishment in this life. But we artists are the culture bearers, the torch bearers. We have not conformed and not given in, and the example we set is a great trouble to the government. So I am denied even a place to work, or the tools, and my most creative period is lost: not written down. I am too desperate and exhausted.

One cannot be an artist unless one is totally free, and one truly free person, one artist, threatens the entire system.

I often live in agony because they permanently black-listed me, and secret accusations which I never heard until recently, destroyed all chance of a normal life. I was thrust into a living death—artistic and emotional death—because I was denied an audience, denied self-expression in this United States of the Soviet Union. "You will never be published again. We can play pretty rough." And I was denied even the chance to survive and work, and the secret false accusations against me made me out as a violent person to cover up for their own theft and dishonesty, their own crimes, making me a target of endless violence and cruelty, a pariah dog cast into the gutter, denied a home, love and denied hope.

Do I have any hope? I've been badly beaten time after time and often gave up wanting to live. I have longed for death. I've had times of intense happiness—moments. I have loved and been loved. I have achieved some fine things—much of what I set out to do, I did, things often far beyond the reach of most humans. I was a hero. I wrote and published books. I taught at Harvard. If death takes me, I will die serene because I have been to the mountaintops and have seen, the promised land as Martin Luther King said, because I knew love but most of all because I <u>tried</u>. I gave my mission all I had even though this terrible handicap of sickness and homelessness, of insecurities, obscurity and opposition hold me back. I tried. I didn't altogether fail. I had so much love in me, so much to give. I have—still—so much more.

In society's terms I failed. I haven't got a pot to piss in. But I'm ready to die now, relatively young. This life is too painful for me. I'm taking my life if there is really no hope. I don't want to be a burden. It's like a cancer patient maintained artificially against his will, so that the medical industrial complex can make more money.

They want us social surplus to die. There's too many people. I often want to die because they have made this life so intolerable for so many of us. But I'm in a chess game with God, and He's left me my Queen. As long as I have that queen, which is what is in my heart, I'll fight on until I'm dead. Fight somehow, resist. I want it on the conscience of this city that they killed one of their best writers. I <u>want</u> to die in the streets, as I am living in the streets, so that perhaps one more martyrdom, one more victim of injustice, one more death—and life—will count for something. That is why Christ died on his cross, and so many others, because life can be too much of a living death otherwise.

My work, my writing, my research is not finished. They don't want me to finish. They want me dead. But perhaps someone will remember Harry, somehow my writing will live, and what I stood for will become known, that I counted for something, that I stood up to be counted, (and perhaps before I die, some lovely girl will give me her love.)

Our oppressors don't want this, so spit in their damn eye and overturn their money tables in the temple as the angry Jesus did. Only then is your soul truly immortal, because you were true to your heart. Hope is what you hope to give to others. Hope is that you try always to win, to do the best you could, to be vindicated, to love, to be loved.

Harrison Edward Livingstone

How many roads
does a man travel
down, before they call
him a "Man?" Many,
many roads; many, many
roads, many roads to get
to the end!!!

I believe in a
"Higher Power" and I
know it works through
each one of us. When
someone hurts us it
seems we take it out
on Those we love most.

Lois Tragesser

FROM REAGAN'S CAMP TO OUR DAILY BREAD

My brother Rod and I left Fort Wayne, Indiana, January 5, 1982 at 2:30 Am, en route to Phoenix, Arizona. We left home for a job a friend had promised us. Rod is eighteen years old and I'm twenty. We were dropped off on Highway 70 West, about fifty miles outside of Indianapolis. We hitched a ride with a trucker to Dallas, and then got a ride with an army recruiter to Gordon, Texas. The next ride took us all the way to Phoenix, Arizona. There, we found out that the man we were going to work for in Phoenix had moved to Texas.

We stayed in a commune camp, otherwise known as Reagan's Camp on the corner of Eighth and Jefferson Streets. People lived in a parking lot out of cars and shanties. Everyday some black people would come by in a truck and drop off food.

We got a job on a ranch in New River, Arizona, forty-five miles north of Phoenix. We stayed there for a week and didn't get paid. So, we took off for Los Angeles, California. It took us eight hours to get a ride out of Tonapah, Arizona. The next day we got a ride to Blythe, California, just three miles west of the California line and a cop stopped us and checked us out. He told us we both had to have ten dollars each in our pockets, or he would arrest us for vagrancy. Since we were broke, we had our Mom wire us twenty dollars. That night we slept in a vacant field because we had to wait until the morning to get the money. The next day we went to a church to seek refuge for the night, but instead ended up going to Las Vegas, Nevada.

We hitch-hiked back to Quartzite, Arizona. A rock and gem show was being held, and we got jobs working at Keasey's Food Concession stand, where I was barbecue cook, and Rod was a grill cook. We were supposed to get twenty dollars a day. Our pay added up to two hundred dollars each, but they said they didn't have enough money to pay us due to lack of sales caused by a rainstorm. So we took a bunch of their meat and sold it to get money for a ticket back to Phoenix. In Phoenix we spent the night in some bushes alongside an "on" ramp.

The next morning we hitched a ride to Tucson, Arizona. There, a nice young lady took us through New Mexico to Anthony, Texas where we spent the night at a Mission. The next day we visited Juarez, Mexico. Then we got a ride with a man going to Orlando, Florida. We figured to get off in Mobile, Alabama, but we found out you could not hitch-hike in Alabama, so we went to Lake City, Florida.

We got a ride with a man going to Rochester, New York. We thought we were lucky, but just South of Manning, South Carolina, at a rest stop, he dumped our stuff out on the roadway and took off without us. A trucker saw this happen and gave us a ride to Manning, South Carolina. We spent nine hours in Manning, before we got a ride to Baltimore, Maryland.

Along the way we heard about the snow storm coming to Baltimore, so we got shelter at the Rescue Mission overnight. We were referred to the Travelers Aid at the Greyhound Bus Station. However, it was not open due to the weather. Someone told us about Our Daily Bread. We went there and had lunch, and that is where we met Mark Bateman. We asked him if we could stay at his place until Monday? He said, "yes" and so that is our story.

Tim
March, 1983

ANDY / E PLURIBUS UNUM / CHECKMATE

I used to see him at the comer of Connecticut and Q in Washington, D.C. An old bearded man, looking a bit like Karl Marx, dressed in shabby, dirty clothes and wearing a pair of heavy mountain-climbing boots. He would be there every afternoon from 3 to 7 pm, pan-handling the young and elegant crowd of 'chic entrepreneurs/lawyers and bureaucrats briskly walking back home after the usual 9-5 paper shuffle of our "busy" nation's capital.

His name was Andy. I would see him on my way to the coffee house where I relaxed in the afternoon over a mug of beer. Occasionally I would push two bits into his palm, and I would feel good. (God would surely remember my generosity.) But sometimes I would walk away a little disturbed. I guess I was afraid and maybe even a bit confused. Perhaps I easily saw myself unwanted, boneless, jobless and dirty like him. It was a scary thought. Didn't I have faith? Then I didn't comprehend how in the "richest" country on earth, an individual could be so poor and destitute and treated with less respect by the Constitution than the morning garbage by the trashmen. It didn't make sense to me and didn't fit in with my concept of democracy, of liberty and most of all, of the right to life.

I remember always wishing I could help Andy more. And I felt a bit ashamed about it. But two bits at a time was really all I could afford. I was having a hard go of it myself, barely making ends meet with my job as a resident manager of an apartment building in the fashionable Adams-Morgan area. It wasn't exactly lucrative employment. Also, I was trying to earn a Master's degree in Agricultural Economics. Then there was my ten year old beat up VW; there was always something wrong with it. So you see there wasn't much I could do to help Andy financially at least. (But what about the forty millionaires in the U.S. Senate?)

As the months passed, I got to know Andy a little better. We would talk on the street corner for a while. He was quite intelligent—no genius mind you, but there was something there. Sometimes I would see him in the coffee house resting from hours of standing on the street and nursing a lukewarm cup of coffee in his weather-rough hands. We would talk a little then. He had very bad teeth and dirty long hair, but always well combed. He had only one set of clothes, those on him, and they were very greasy looking and smelled bad.

I learned how he lived when he wasn't at the street comer. I suppose I was curious—that's maybe the main reason I asked him those questions. And there was something incomprehensible too which prompted me—how could the "greatest" society on earth permit one of its members to live on the streets like that?

Andy usually spent his nights awake in 24 hour coffee shops near bus stations. From six in the morning till early afternoon he would sleep in a doorway, a park bench, or an abandoned row house, wherever he felt "safe" and "comfortable" at the moment. In the late afternoon and early evenings, he would panhandle the sidewalk mob of well-to-do Washingtonians.

Andy had no family. He was alone. An American alone! That is a strange concept! Don't you see? What does *E Pluribus Unum* on our Great Seal mean? "Out of many, one." But probably it means very little since there are three or four hundred thousand street people like Andy in this Capitalistic Republic. They're living the street comers of our urban ghettoes: proles walking in a Babel-like forest of skyscrapers in search of a dream maybe, along with a simple two-bits for a tin of hot coffee. Or maybe they are just walking or sitting in dilapidated doorways waiting for Godot.

Andy told me he was waiting for a check from the Supreme Court that would set him up for life. I thought he was crazy. But I remember that he didn't smile when he said it, or didn't laugh like a maniac. Then he told me its amount, quite a large sum. "The total: <u>Justice</u>, and the bank: an institution called <u>Truth</u>."

One day Andy disappeared from the street comer of Connecticut and Q. I never found out what happened to him, but I hope he got that check he was waiting for—for his sake and for mine.

Marc Grabowski

the raft

Truly a vacuumed feeling about
Little pebbles of disarray: The unarmed man
Slow winter of regret
No niceties. Just cold
I cannot live this way in the drone of Low mourn
I cannot spare the blood, the draining of the vein
True life is toasty and on its heels.
It is brushed and swept and clean
Suddenly the mountain ranges and we have peaked again.
We then smile.
Oh, how we feel the glad and with the spoil all gone
But the raft, the raft...
Does it come in again?
Travis Johns

HALFWAY HOUSE

Charles Village House

August 27, 1978

Why I've done that before I sighed quietly
Hugging all of them with my eyes;
One who sat behind her clothes and yawned.
She ate tomatoes like they were diamonds.
When the doors are not open I enter
Under the guise of a visitor.

Touching the cloth I remember raising my
Hand in despair while they sighed too
Come with us and be with us. You are one of
Us with your sad eyes and your shaking hand
Back to that year ago
When I painted the basement room.
I will sleep again tonight while their T.V.
News and cigarette butts trail smokey messages.
Truth in wondering what lies to believe.
Believing all of them.
Secretly I was glad at the holes in the
Wall and the stoic faces. "Oh, what we've been through."
Oh, what we've been through washing dishes.
Wandering about the city and finally,
Coming home once again, Knowing it to be true.

Ken Girard.

JOHN'S WHEREABOUTS

Once upon a time, long, long ago, there was a little boy who had a yo-yo. He liked to play with it so much that it broke in two pieces and fell apart. He tried to put it back together again, but he couldn't because it was broken. He tried several methods to put it back together but he couldn't.

He loved life and art work, but he couldn't find what to do with all his treasures, and so he ended up in a grave, trying to get out. A little angel came by and blessed him with life and loved him so much, and he let him go into a new world. After that, he became a little baby, and his mother loved him a lot.

He is like a dummy that keeps popping out of his grave and doesn't want to go back. They tried buzzes on him, and he still wouldn't go; he loved life dearly and wouldn't go back again.

That is the end.

John Vereen

THIEF

I come like a thief in the night to steal the fine things in life
    you don't give me
    your stereo, Porsche and jewelry
    treasures of your mundane existence
    taken and sold, supporting my habits
    whiskey, heroin, cheap thrills of the chase
    to be hunter and prey
    to feel alive
    the difference separating our twin roads
    your bright toys
    my grey world
    I saw your 100 points/TILT smile on the magazine
    playing with some pretty boys
    name-brand, jet-set. neon bright
    those flawless teeth
    a fortune removed from my molted mirror
    the cavity and stain of my most gleeful mouth
    I'm done, you're snorting coke
    the waste is the same
    deciphering the center spread, you still smiled the same
    inside I felt empty
    cancel my subscription, break that false image
    I've found the thief
    it was me, and the goods I had stolen were meaningless.

Carol Garcia

A PSYCHIATRISTS' DISCOURSE
RUDELY INTERRUPTED BY A PATIENT

"What symphonies
do catatonics hear
as they weave and bob
to an invisible lyre"

"do colours burst
on the blank screen
of catatonic eyes"

"do catatonics run
through fields of praise
unshackled by our lack of passionate desire"
"are roses velvet
in catatonic hands
their perfumes redolent
of celestial fire"
i know
because i walked
out of the barbed-wire fence
of an educated mind
into the frenzy of
the night
with winged feet
and high heart
i laughed
wore next to nothing
passed through walls

out of the city
out of the daylight world
into the madhouse
staring
stark and stiff
my soul sailed
into the glory
without fear
feverish and fey

i know
that one can live on dreams
i almost died
but didn't
i am here
a testimony of light
a child of ice and ire
god-intoxicated ,
existentially liberated
beaten
sedated
almost hated
and free
as the wind is free
to play with children's hair
and kiss their faces unafraid
untouchable
unreachable
and wild

Theodora Stanley Snyder

CRY OF THE SOCIAL BUTTERFLY

My wings are purple, lavender in places
I am a creature of many faces
All of them varied, unique
A different one to whoever I speak

As I dip and soar on gossamer wings
My heart sings as it cries
Am I one to be despised?

Some, many think me vain
Yet only I know the pain
I feel when I am alone
I did not choose my destiny
I carry my cocoon with me
As I flit from soul to soul
Always trying to stay whole
When I am alone.

Dianna West

PIGEONS ON STONE

The sky has become grey with pigeon's dust
Dusting the plaza they walk delicately
Over stones and crumbs of soot
Pecking rhythmically like tin soldiers
in a War of mind and body and red beveled legs

Without destination they perch until I
Tap the window. Again off and floating
Sullen, forlorn, alone fighting over the
Whole wheat bread from my sandwich.

Ken Girard

ANAIS NIN

Anais Nin, where have you been?
You left me agog, awash in your images
so close to my soul.

I pick up your books and put them down
each time more furtively
Each time my world is eclipsed
into yours.

I am agog, awash in your images
Yours so close to mine.

M.F.

UNTITLED

Shades of crimson dangle along the setting sun.
The handsome stranger struts on by, thinking he's the one,
Lovers lie along the grass and speak their tender words.

Winged Scavengers fly the sunset trails preying on smaller birds.
The populace like actors in a long forgotten play,
Wake to shades of purple and do these things every day.

Vagabonds and jokers smile beneath the pale moon's glow,
Not trying to find the answers to things they'll never know.

Larry Minitor

HOW TO FEEL

At certain times I anxiously await a feeling of inner acceptance. In order to feel this way I must look at myself, another persons' perspective of me, which will at times boost my inner esteem, and self-image.

/* Cause— my low self-image
/* Effect—constantly asking questions
/paranoia/

My feelings of paranoia stem from delusions of grandiosity which causes me to become manic at a high level of adrenaline, which when I drink coffee causes me to think in introverted retrospect. I feel that I must make up for delusions by feelings of guilt.

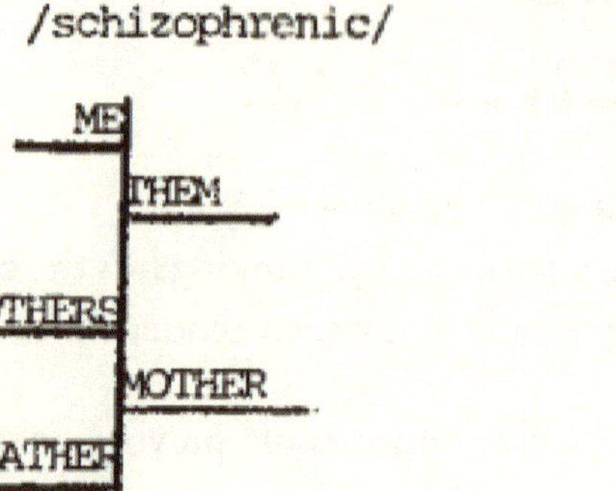

Shannon Power's Poetry
John 3:16

HALFWAY HOUSE

All or none
overture of tears
swaddled anxieties
Mother I love you, But if I can't have you,
then nobody can,
cause nobody cares, cause nobody cares
cause nobody, nobody
wants a mind like that anyway
I once was lost,
and now I've gotten used to it.
I once was lost,

and now I've gotten used to it,
and I'm gonna keep on using it
and I'm gonna feel good.
My ship was sinking in the night
and a voice told me how to breathe water
so I walked to the other side,
where there was dry land,
and I got lost all over again.
The doctor looked at my dreams
and told me drugs and pussy was my downfall,
and I asked him, I said doctor
if I stop eating drugs and using pussy
will I get better, he said no
but if a problem rises, swallow two Stelazine
and call me later tonight.
So I got another doctor who wasn't trying to get me
She injected me with twenty-five Milligrams of Thorazine
a hundred mgs. of Prolixin and thirty-five mgs
of some new psychotropic, handed me a mirror
and said see, now you look just like everybody else, all
you need is a suit and a briefcase.
My father had told me, I was never gonna be anybody
and I was never gonna amount to anything,
so I asked my mother what he meant,
scratching her ass she said I don't know son
ask your father
Fresh out of the hospital
Fresh out of the hospital, and I was feeling
fresh out of the hospital, and fresh -out of personality
My name is edgar rice burroughs and I want to live
in your jungle with all the other animals,
I've got a masters in Special Ed, and I don't like

masturbating all by myself, and I'm screaming
I'm a screamer, and I need your house, I'm a screamer,
and I need your help. I'm a screamer, and I want
to go all the way, won't you please
help me escape, this lack of reality.

John Murro

TO MY LOST FRIEND

Oh, my friend; you asked me not what I see
tho I will tell you so, and by so doing, speak more of me,
You are a river rat on hamster row, an unclean thing full of
pomp
and show. Upon your head, I see the Cardinal's crown, the
scarlet
heart, pierced ruby red jewel, the dripping frown....
of Kings and men and wars and terrible deeds, you sow, you
reap
lay waste your seeds, chop off a head, rip out a heart....
make doubt, make fear, serenity of God, depart.

Thy creature of the night, what day blindness assails you,
that you cannot see the greatness of the smallest acorn,
such is man, of woman born. Your seed, it searches, like a
dandelion
puffed on the wind, lands on some poppyseed flower; illusions
grand delusions, dwelling within; you creep about in day, the
light
assails you, it chases you, picks you out of corners,
shows your nightmare ridden face to the crowd, you shout,
you spit,
you writhe and snake about...and still no mercy from the
crowd.

You pant, you gasp for air, from all this torment; you find
relief
inside a jail, imprisonment? You scoff, you scorn, you rage,
You're not reborn....you're lost....No rose!....No!....Nothing....
but a thorn! Pray thee to God, to open up your heart, to put

the Spirit's flame inside your head; to pierce your hardened heart
with ray of hope, the son, Christ's blood again begins to flow,
to bleed anew....the ROSE ..... where did it go?

Paula

CITY POEM

callous strangers passing by
no time to touch them
this is because so many walk fast
wanting not to be known
one hundred and five blocks
an unzipped wino stops, offering to share our lunch
limbless beggars lined up on a certain street
looking like it costs to pass them
like trolls
a troll train
–just keep walking

after the pace other strange types
street people, a screamer
the black voodoo schizo with a purple wig who "rushed" us
a block of children in wheelchairs, a grisly postage stamp oasis
I thought
then a melted face gestures for us to move aside
with characteristic city rudeness
she startled John, but I saw it coming
getting pebbled by leering beef-cakes
classic grade B movie Italian punk hoods
truck drivers who screeched to red at the very last moment
I wonder if they do it every Thursday 9 to 5

thereby keeping down the pedestrian population
with so many people it doesn't seem to matter
I felt safe with friends until I saw them walking close
to my sides with the shocked look out
like a bun hugs a frank in a hungry cafe
one little store sold my balance back
buying something soft to lean into
some brushes: a purpose
not like the runaway kid of ten years ago who felt oppressed by
these crowds, shuffled by this city

already bruised in the head
remembering these faces
grasping at already forgotten details
anonymous features
from corner to comer we walked with their feet
(we had to, to keep from falling)
as we passed, I heard a Mexican tell two others
in Mexican, "tourist"
imported Mayan sentinels?
to say the city is dying, the scale gone
large buildings caging human trust, venting suspicion
not getting involved as a way of coping, a way of going on
the survivalists' slogan "I live in N.Y."
heartlessness: this is our sickness.

Carol Garcia

HALFWAY HOUSE

Dedicated to Vishnu, the Sustainer

Age 30: Time of maturing and flowering of eyes and heart; awareness of
on Earth standing,
    not alone.
    Place: Halfway house
    Event: Street madness turning into reasoned sanity

Scene 1: Dawning awareness of Baltimore city as well
planned, with streets patterned (by Catholics) into the form
of a cross; Baltimore street and Charles street forming as
crossbeams.

–hours of library study and history of the Lords of Baltimore.

Help: coming through acceptance by society as having a mind
and intellect, as having a head on my shoulders.

Chores: hours of walking tours, church visiting, and visiting
of homes, parks, Masonic temples, and city wide historical
institutions, attendance at craft fairs and inner harbor ethnic
festivals.

Result: a dawning awareness of the overreaching patterns in Urban
sprawl.

Secondary result: A finding of myself emerging from a low
dipped valley ground rising to a crest where I could perceive
the broad picture of things.

And emergence of the broad picture; expanding awareness of life's scope and grandeur.

Cinemas, and photography, art museums, and the Etta Cohen collection of European paintings, one Baltimore link with the larger world.

Another scene: a nice day spent visiting the Baltimore arts Tower,

Aspirations growing.

Another: visit to the Theatre Project, and awakening interest in music and the Theatre.

Acceptance: of life's hum-drum dull moments as sacred in their own right, and the sanctity of daily routine. A growing feeling of life's oneness.

Blossoming: lotus flower emerging from the mud, and simultaneous visit of the Nam Myoho Kenge Kyo Buddhist chanters to the otherwise Christian halfway house.

Event: A growing of life force in dimensions of intelligence.

A graded quickening and growing curiosity for life's beauty and infinite possibilities.

Helped along by: sports, voluntary work in a children's center – and broadening impressions of positive action.

Increasing taste for life; for life's simply joys and flavours like eating crabs and sipping the foam on a glass of beer, like dreaming of old days and clipper ships crossing ocean brine.

Increasing enjoyment in friends, and dear ones, in a trusted relationship

with one of the opposite sex, in picnics and woodland country.

scenes and baseball games and sports and ideas and philosophical

points of view which drive life's energy.

Finally, a kick out the front door and a heme opening up for a time with accepting people (of a faith) and a blossoming acceptance of being "above board" and oh my! here's life!!!

Conclusions: Halfway houses are time of filling, receiving, and way station.

Time for half of life and half play.

World of cards, games, social recreation, and expansion time-out

before tackling life's false/real world problems.

Like Vishnu, the sustainer, a sustaining moment and pause to receive life's beauty, and directivity, and strength in a world gone mad:

a rest haven or sanity.

Memories of Mehere Baba's ashrams and His work through love

with the mad in India.

A watchtower for future planning, a window on the world, and a door to future eternity and life's big picture for one and all.

by Bob Fish

END OF THE CITY

OLYMPOS

Olympus a far crest
tumultuous and winding
veined as the stone hand of Nemesis
reposes in the crevices
of the mind
in the staid and imposing
terror of Olympus
only gulls reign
this vile place
winging and winding upward
hilarious above
the curious stonework
of gods long scattered
from the crypt of the angry temple
where the dizzying height
intoxicates with dread
i walk
here gods have been flung down
passionless gulls
scream in derision above
the upward foot path
where the laurel sits
heavy upon the soul and dead
i celebrate with a wearisome ecstasy
the fell height
mark you the dire echo
of the gulls cry
the climb that has bent me
ruthlessly
and the flight

into the realm of the furies
majesty
Olympus

Theodora Snyder

SUSPENSION

There's no room for wine and cheese
and stoved warm shacks
in this barren icecapade
Where cities heats and sounds
blow up cold silent nights
There's hardly room for oranges and brandy
and what makes a day a day
it seems these days are only made
for getting done before tomorrow
And the thin lines grew thicker and turned to wrinkles
before I felt the smoothness that had crept away
I wonder what kept you running all this time
Broken mirrors reflecting a somewhat
curious mind
and seven years of bad luck seems hardly worth the risk
The shift is cool
and smooth and clear and changes
with the tide
and widens that crowded space
it reflects a more direct channel of pure water
There's no more room for snow-lit evergreens
or paintings that mirror their sparkles
That's all gone now but I will always like lavender
and tasting grapes
living between today and tomorrow

Becky Bauknight

APOCALYPSE

Morsels of the sun
Die in syncopation
While the sun goddess weeps her last song
The plague has begun
People in plastic bags heading toward the city dump.
I lock myself in my room
Waiting to die
My posters are tired now
A bush in a landscape winks at me
I gather up my cotton rags and silk for
the long journey
We have used this one up
Discarding it like laundry
No one comes to clean.
My eyes are brown now
As the sun
Our only loved one is leaving us behind
Out in the cold, the roommate
Refused admittance moans over the phone.
Bemoan the landscape and the smoke from the
factory rancid.
I have watched the faces wither into
The ocean like sugar melts into
Sand to specs lying no
Where in particular.

Ken Girard

SEA URCHIN

I watch you from a distance long slender legs
small shoulders tanned to a toasty brown.
A reflection of another child. A millennium of summer past.
Dodging the waves, sandpiper style
to gather treasures from the sea.
Smiling even when broken fragments
are the day's catch. When the sun softens his
glaring, we walk home together as I wonder,
will you watch your sea urchin with older eyes
as I do—lovingly.

Dianna West

DESCENT

Seeking peace in oneness
the cast-out and the homeless
drifting downward through the
waters to the sand

We seek the lowest level
in the dark and quiet sea
in the bosom of the Mother of the race.
Chant the ancient hymns
and sing us down below
your voices will accompany us
on the journey.
Aside we cast our garments
and begin our long descent to join
the Old Ones at the bottom
where the footing is sure

ANON. LEPER

APOCALYPSE OF THE CITIES

I leave Baltimore at noon, on holiday, circumambulating Beltway in car, sending motorized salutations to this concrete madness; heading north on the throughway.

By evening I reach Philadelphia; I talk with a street walker and hear of her weary travels from New York, to Washington, to Philly: keeping peace in city jungle through cash on the line togetherness.

Philadelphia, jumble of Park concerts, downtown office buildings, and large ghetto sprawl....variation of Baltimore.

Night spent in Philly hotel; because one has to unwind slowly from the city, like drug addiction or an alcohol binge. Already I have two wisps of nature; driving over the Delaware and Susquehanna Rivers from the toll road bridge.

Next day to Atlantic City and first dip in the ocean, foamy spray in sight of Caesar's Palace. Water curving around cramped rehabilitating feet; being simultaneously roasted hot summer sun on sand, and a walk on the Boardwalk.

I sip ice tea in sight of the ocean, letting the element water do its work, washing away the grime of city living. I can only bear two hours of Atlantic City. The ocean relaxes me, but the high rise hotel, casino city is jangling.... a strange juxtaposition of city and sea.

Next stop, Seascape, New Jersey, a quiet ocean resort town; the first stages of entering into the world of nature and two more swims of being tossed around by the ocean.

I feel the majesty of the ocean; an allegory of all life force....waves of ocean as waves of life, ever advancing to the shore. Now approaching.....one after another the waves leave no roan for thought of negativity.

I revel in the ocean waves. Jumping over a breaker, diving under another. Feeling joy to be able to stand firm against their flux. Enjoying the rapport with my fellow swimmers. Until I cannot remember a time when I had any other struggle in life than to battle and meet these watery forces.

And then, ocean fears: the power of the undertow, the danger of being dragged out to sea, and crisscross waves which can topple a man regardless of fame or accomplishments..... and pull him out to sea.

By Wednesday I find myself standing under a concrete shelter in a driving rain, watching the ocean waves being shipped into a mid-summer storm.

The driving white tipped foam brings back memories of childhood days when I built sand castles on the shore, and watched the water destroy than. This memory now forming itself into an allegory of nature's power to destroy man's creations and the cities.

Standing in the rain, I relax, and give in, breathing in the low hung salt sea air, hitting bottom, journey's end, with release of all striving for one moment. I acknowledge that I am beaten down man's artificiality and the cities? that I am poisoned by it..... taken far, far away from nature where one is at one with the All and with his own heart.

Far away, from job, friends and loved ones... dearest beloved one; and left in a stark seascape setting which if I had only kept my hold on its pure un-trammeled beauty twenty-four hours a day I would have that which I have not.

—yet, I could not think of a summer, save when I was young, that it was not so.

Soft sea, signpost of that which is ever pure, ever untrammeled. Breathing breath of life. Prana.... feeling ever renewed; strength of the Beyond entering in.

Leaving Monmouth Beach, I travel on to New York City; by-passing most of the city via the Hudson Parkway and George Washington Bridge, I witness this concrete megalith, steel girded cathedral, conglomeration of noise and haste, and travel on to New England via the New England throughway.

Riding in my car, I experience a state of shock and wave of relief to breathe in the first breath of fresh New England air; and be re-in-touch with a natural setting.

Friends await me in Boston which I surmise as the city with the most refreshing air; being as it is closest to our Northern extremes.

It is a six hour drive along concrete highways piled with snow in winter now reflecting refracted neat patterns in the warm surface air.

The highway passes through Hartford, past tall bleak buildings, associated by most with insurance and banking interests. I think of Hartford life. "Is this life?" Or city madness death?

The pace quickens. I reach my final destination, point of farthest distance, another city.... Boston, Massachusetts; city madness muted by northern air. Culturally rich, packed haphazardly into surrounding urban sprawl. And then, I return in one day and night's drive to the city of origin, Baltimore.

II.

Relaxing in my suburban apartment I ask myself, can this be man's monument love that we pack ourselves like sardines into a huge cramped can; a bear hug of urban togetherness.... rather titan spreading ourselves across the vastness of earth's countryside? Or is it madness that we bow our heads oblivious to the immense universal cosmic sea in which we live, in our attempts to be near one another. I gaze at the city.

Oh! rectangular square steel and concrete pillars; walled off sectors of madness. Bundle of intensely impacted and compacted activity.... I weep.

Oh! air of God, fresh blue wisps of clouds, and fire of sun to look down on such dark urbane madness.

From below, rising rectangles of concrete steel, and the proud architects who raised these immortal monuments to man's strength, man's adventure, his stupidity and pride, his ingenious lust for space, and his unnatural separation from life's flow ..... and stubborn refusal to reemerge.

Triangles, squares, circles; our cities are a bouquet of Euclidian geometry. And yet, Pythagoras might turn in his grave to see his forms used so.

These immortal buildings, which have yet been toppled by earthquake and fire, flood and tornadoes; and like their ancestors the Greek Parthenon and Reman edifices will be worn down by the toll of time.

They are no more secure than the sea-side sand castles of my youth.

III

A conflict approaches the apocalypse. Man cannot forget nature, as nature creates man. Our Earth and its natural resources can be stretched only so far.

Predictions of old rise before me: The Millennium, the Second Coming, The Messiah, Quiamet, the Primal Dm sound of Hinduism, the destruction of Shiva; hints of the solution.

Shiva....the son of Brahma; third of the Tri-Partite Indian deity of Creator, Sustainer, and Dissolver; the destroyer of all things created.

Destruction of that which is passing, destruction of that which is annoying, destruction of that which gives disease, destruction of that which causes desire, and separation, destruction of that which is filthy and unwholesome, destruction of that which is false or futile, destruction of that which is not God.

All this world passes, this illusion, this cosmic show, this Maya, this nothing into Nothing.

All this heartache disappears, all this suffering has to end. All this confusion will cease; even these words have an end. Cities too must have an end; pain of city life, heartache of city existence, for.... at the very last....ONLY GOD IS ETERNAL.

BIOGRAPHIC SKETCHES:

When Bruce has a place, he studies chess and draws. He has done expert bird watching with his father, a biologist. Bruce recently attempted some pick-up work but wasn't paid by his employer. Bruce is now on the street.

Joe pushes a heavy wheeled cart of discarded items around the North Avenue/Jones Falls area. He is very timid and will hardly speak. He hasn't been seen since mid-winter.

Clem wrote his fictional piece, "My Little Spot" while hospitalized for frostbite last winter. Clem says the hospital refused to take him twice until it was too late, and he had to have his toes amputated.

Lois spends much of her time walking the streets, though she now lives in a boarding home. At various places she visits, she leaves behind her writings on small index cards.

Marc, a graduate of Georgetown, found himself homeless in Washington, D.C., and later lived out of his car in the Baltimore area. Marc is a former peace corps volunteer, and is fluent in French and Japanese.

Harry, graduate of Harvard, author, and researcher of the Kennedy Assassination, has been living out of his car for most of the past two years.

An unknown young man was found frozen on a sheet of ice under the Howard Street bridge last winter. A priest arrived in time to administer the man last rites before he was wrapped up in a cellophane bag. This elegy was written by a former "street person" who heard of the death.

BENEATH THE RAGS...

Baltimore Evening Sun Article: Nov, 28, 1983

Poetry

Beneath the rags lies a soul ready, willing to take flight

By Carl Schoettler
Evening Sun Staff

Learn from
the little
children
the way they act

The Ball
rolled down
the steps
of its
free will
how did it
do it? There
was no wind.

The lady who wrote those verses is very, very carefully washing her feet in a basin on the floor at Mike Susko's small St. Paul Street apartment. She spent the night on her feet after a big, fat, ugly guard forced her out of the ladies room of a downtown parking garage. It's important to take care of your feet when you live on the street. And this poet lives on the street.

Her name is Lois Tragesser. She usually slips her latest work under Susko's door. He's editor of "Street Images 1983," a compilation of writing by street people, people who live in halfway houses and the people who love and care for them.

Tragesser does most of her writing at the Enoch Pratt library.

"That's a church," she says. "The answer to everything is in there."

She talks with a kind of sly, meandering brilliance while she very slowly washes her foot. She's got one shoe on and one shoe off. Her shoes are in pretty fair shape, but she says they're no good. They've got plastic rubber soles and that'll burn your 'er.

"Remember when you were five?" she asks. "Who did you admire? Who did you despise? Who were you afraid of?"

She's insistent. She really wants an answer.

"Because that's the most important part of your life."

Susko's sitting cross-legged on his desk, just listening. He's a counselor in a halfway house, and a lot of what he does is listen.

Tragesser's one of 10 street people who've contributed to Street Images. Eleven people wrote pieces for the Halfway House section, and another five did works for the concluding part called End of the City, visions of nuclear apocalypse, and a city reborn.

"Just living in the neighborhood is one reason for the book," Susko says. "Walking around. These are the things that are there."

Benjamin Board and Shawn McNeill, two kids from this neighborhood around North and St. Paul, did art work, and so did some of the authors and a Maryland Institute student named John Herman.

"I had a lot of help," says Susko, a compassionate, self-effacing guy who can display surprising strength when his principles are challenged.

"Our society has conditioned us in a thousand subtle ways to believe that certain people should be avoided," he says in a statement about Street Images. "That certain people are unfit.

"We imagine their existence as reduced to begging—that nothing else goes on. But beneath those beggar's rags lies a human soul like yours and mine, and if we approach him as a brother and equal that soul can take flight. This journal is witness to that tenet."

He mostly had to go out and collect pieces from the street people. He stopped a guy named Red Top on Charles Street near Mount Vernon Place.

See STREET, D6, Col. 1

By Richard Childress—Evening Sun Staff

Mike Susko talks with Lois Tragesser about some of her writing and that of other street people.

Rags hide a soul that's ready to fly

STREET, From D1

"And he wrote something then and there. He must have trusted me. Nobody usually goes up to these people and says please write me something."

Red Top is a red-headed crewcut sailor sort of guy. His work is called "Life in the Streets."

Every day is the same for us poor people. We have to struggle to make it from day to day. We have to bum some money to eat and get everything we need.

From the time we get up in the morning it is a struggle to live. My day is the same every day. Nothing changes at all.

The only day that changes is when I get my check. Then I have the money to get what I want.

A guy named "Joe" gave Susko two wonderful paragraphs called "Memory."

It was a sunny day, very bright, about 90 degrees. In the sunlight by the shore I was just getting tired of fishing. I was going to stop fishing and about one minute later, the fish got caught. It was fighting very hard and I could hardly take him. On shore, he moved around and then got tired. I tied fishing string to his mouth and took him home.

My mother had bought fish that same day, and it was the same type I had just caught. It was a funny coincidence that happened 20 years ago."

"If you can imagine somebody bundled up so you can't see their face, you have Joe," Susko says. "And he shies away and he sort of recedes into the background as you approach. And then sit down and ask him to tell you a story, to tell you something about his life. And it was a cold, gray day. I asked him to tell me a story, tell me anything that happened to you.

"He's got all his stuff there," Susko says. "He's sort of leaning against his cart, a grocery cart full of all sorts of items, discarded items, newspapers, cans, sometimes food."

Joe told his story of the funny coincidence of the fishes that happened 20 years ago.

"I wrote it down then," Suskos says. "When you think about this guy walking around in all this gloom and he's got this story in him. The remarkable thing is it's an image of hope and that's what I was looking for."

Lois Tregaster finishes washing

her feet and pulls back on her two pair of socks and her ill-shod shoes.

She's a very handsome woman. Her face is burnished and weathered like a piece of old ivory lost outdoors. She's thin and wiry and her hands are strong and embossed with veins.

She's wearing two pairs of pants, a sweater, a man's shirt and a sweatshirt with the sleeves cut off that says "Smokin' with Winston." She found the sweatshirt in an alley this morning.

"It was turned inside out," she says. "I said I'm going to put this on. We did things like that. We put clothes out on a bench for anybody that might need them. Some people, they put good clothes in garbage cans.

"I met James coming out of the alley," she says. "James was in Crownsville with me. He ain't a very good-looking man. He ain't got any upper teeth. I saw James right after I got this.

"Here's James and this other guy. I said James do you have enough money for a cup of coffee. He said no but here's five cigarettes. He gave me five cigarettes."

Tregasser smokes and drinks coffee but she says she leaves alcohol alone. She rolls her own mostly, out of Bugler tobacco when she's got it, out of butts when she doesn't, and any kind of paper, even tiny squares of old newspapers.

"I been awake all night," she says, "awake all night. There were many of us on the street last night."

She was in a parking garage near Charles and Saratoga for awhile.

"I went in because it was cold," she says. "I went into this parking garage ladies room. I was sitting there, just thinking. After a while this guy's in pounding on the door. He says get the hell out of there. He's old and he's fat and he's just as mean as he can be.

"Well, I left there and believe me I was freezing. I don't know what time it was. See, I don't keep track of time.

"I guess I went uptown," she says, "or I went downtown to The Block.

"My problem is getting money for coffee. For some ungodly reason people don't want to buy you a cup of coffee. You stop somebody on the street and ask them for a cup of coffee you'd think you're asking them for a million dollars.

"I don't drink alcohol. I have tasted it. I don't like it. I'm a coffee drinker.

"Smoke and drink coffee," she says, "and get yourself something to eat and keep your eye on the cops."

Good advice.

And you can get Street Images and more wisdom from the down side of life and meet the authors at a signature party from 2 p.m. to 4 p.m. Dec. 3 at the Peabody Book Store, 913 N. Charles St.

Also by Michael A. Susko

The Dreaming Series
Sleek Back
Streak and Cave Bear Dreaming
Moby and Marsupial Mole Dreaming

Worlds to the Side
Down Below and the Archon's Castle
Up Above and the Runaway
Across the Gulf and Journey Into Un-Time
On the Bay and a Wild Child Found
In the Wild and Do One Wild Thing
On the Mountain and Two Are Missing
To the Beginning and Journey Through Here

Standalone
The Little People
Animal Spell
Child of the Elements
The Firekeeper
Transformational Stories: Voices for True Healing in Mental Health

Watch for more at https://www.allroneofus.com/.

About the Author

Michael Susko, M.S in Counseling Psychology, has been active for several years in advocacy for re-envisioning mental health care. Attending conferences and workshops, he often presented on the meaning of symbolic experiences. In 1991 he edited *Cry of the Invisible*, a collection of oral histories of persons, homeless or psychiatrically labeled. For several years he served on the board for Maryland Disability Rights, to insure the rights of the disabled. The editor has also published works in psychology, evolutionary biology, and creative fiction.

Read more at https://www.allroneofus.com/.